ANCIENT CIVILIZATIONS

Ancient Egyptians

by Anita Ganeri

COMPASS POINT BOOKS MINNEAPOLIS, MINNESOTA

First American edition published in 2007 by
Compass Point Books
3109 West 50th St., #115
Minneapolis, MN 55410

ANCIENT EGYPTIANS
was produced by
David West Children's Books
7 Princeton Court
55 Felsham Road
London SW15 1AZ

Illustrator: Peter Wilks
Designer: Gary Jeffrey
Editors: Kate Newport, Robert McConnell
Page Production: Ellen Schoefield and Bobbie Nuytten
Content Adviser: T. G. Wilfong, Ph.D.,
  Associate Professor of Egyptology,
  University of Michigan

Visit Compass Point Books on the Internet at
www.compasspointbooks.com
or e-mail your request to
custserv@compasspointbooks.com

Library of Congress Cataloging-in-Publication Data
Ganeri, Anita, 1961-
    Ancient Egyptians / by Anita Ganeri.—1st American ed.
      p. cm.—(Ancient civilizations)
    Includes bibliographical references and index.
    ISBN-13: 978-0-7565-1645-1 (hardcover)
    ISBN-10: 0-7565-1645-5 (hardcover)
    ISBN-13: 978-0-7565-1955-1 (paperback)
    ISBN-10: 0-7565-1955-1 (paperback)
    1. Egypt—Civilization—To 332 B.C.—Juvenile literature.
I. Title. II. Series: Ancient civilizations (Minneapolis, Minn.)
  DT61.G33 2006
  932—dc22   2006002990

Contents

The Egyptians

The civilization of ancient Egypt was one of the first and greatest in the world. From its small beginnings about 5,000 years ago, it became powerful and lasted almost 3,000 years. Although the Egyptians lived so long ago, we know a lot about their lives.

Look out for this man digging up interesting items from the past, like this Egyptian ankh, which was an amulet.

Who Were the Ancient Egyptians?

The ancient Egyptian civilization began as a group of villages built along the banks of the Nile River. Slowly, these became two kingdoms—Upper and Lower Egypt. It is said that King Menes of Upper Egypt united them about 5,000 years ago.

For the ancient Egyptians, the desert lying on either side of the Nile River was such a dangerous and lonely place that it was believed to be full of demons.

Much of what we know about the ancient Egyptians comes from the tombs of kings and nobles. The walls of tombs were covered in plaster, and then pictures of people and gods were drawn on top. These pictures were to help the tomb's owner through the afterlife.

Egyptian artists had to follow a strict set of rules in their work. First, a grid was marked on the wall to help the artists get the right shapes. Then they made a sketch that was checked by the chief artist before color and detail were added.

An Egyptian artist might practice on a broken piece of pottery before drawing an object on the tomb wall.

The Egyptian World

Egyptian merchant ship

MEDITERRANEAN SEA

PALESTINE

The pyramids at Giza

Giza •
• Memphis

• Akhetaten

NILE RIVER

• Karnak
• Thebes

RED SEA

Fishing on the Nile

Storing grain

Abu Simbel •

Nubian soldier

Temple boat

• Kerma
• Napata

NUBIA

Temple of Ramses II at Abu Simbel

The Egyptian World

Ancient Egypt was located along the Nile River. The ancient Egyptians called their country Black Land. Each year, the Nile flooded and left behind rich, black soil that was good for farming. The Nile also provided an easy way to travel on boats.

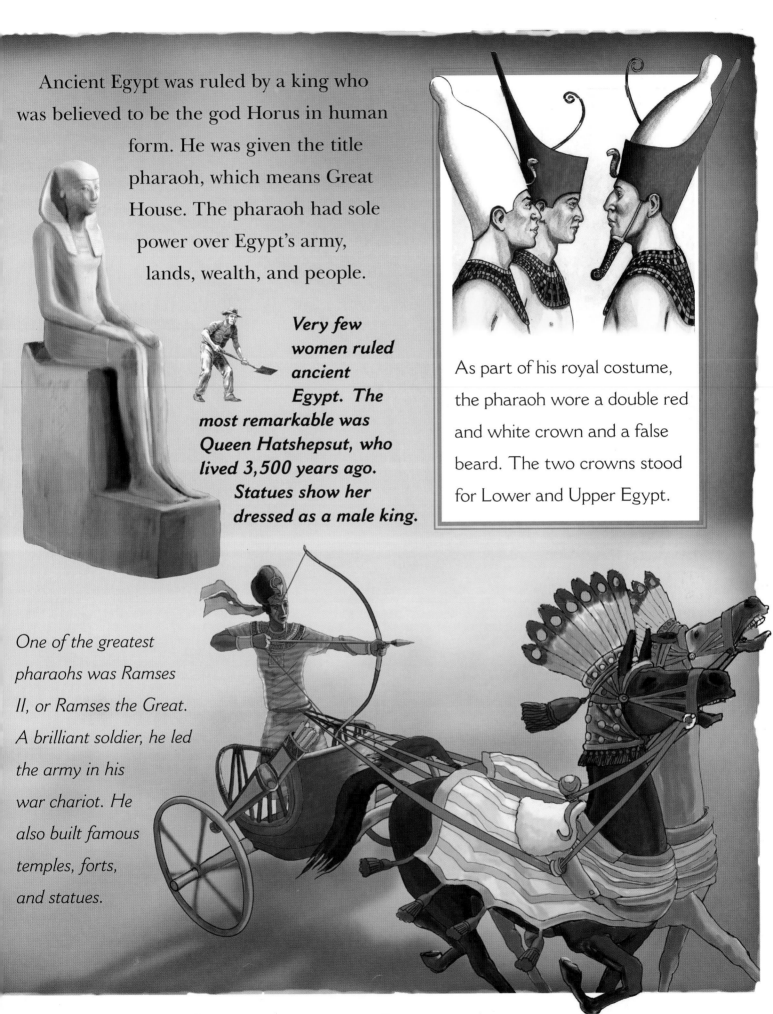

Ancient Egypt was ruled by a king who was believed to be the god Horus in human form. He was given the title pharaoh, which means Great House. The pharaoh had sole power over Egypt's army, lands, wealth, and people.

Very few women ruled ancient Egypt. The most remarkable was Queen Hatshepsut, who lived 3,500 years ago. Statues show her dressed as a male king.

As part of his royal costume, the pharaoh wore a double red and white crown and a false beard. The two crowns stood for Lower and Upper Egypt.

One of the greatest pharaohs was Ramses II, or Ramses the Great. A brilliant soldier, he led the army in his war chariot. He also built famous temples, forts, and statues.

Gods and Goddesses

Ancient Egyptians worshipped many gods and goddesses. They believed that the gods watched over them and looked after every part of the world, life, and death. Some were linked with tasks such as farming and crafts. Many were linked with animals and were pictured with animals' heads.

1. **Ra**—*sun god*

2. **Osiris**—*god of the dead*

3. **Isis**—*wife of Osiris and goddess of crafts*

4. **Horus**—*royal god and son of Osiris and Isis*

5. **Anubis**—*god of embalming*

6. **Bastet**—*cat goddess*

7. **Set**—*god of storms and deserts*

The ancient Egyptians built many temples for the gods. These were believed to be the gods' homes on Earth. Only priests and priestesses were allowed inside the temples.

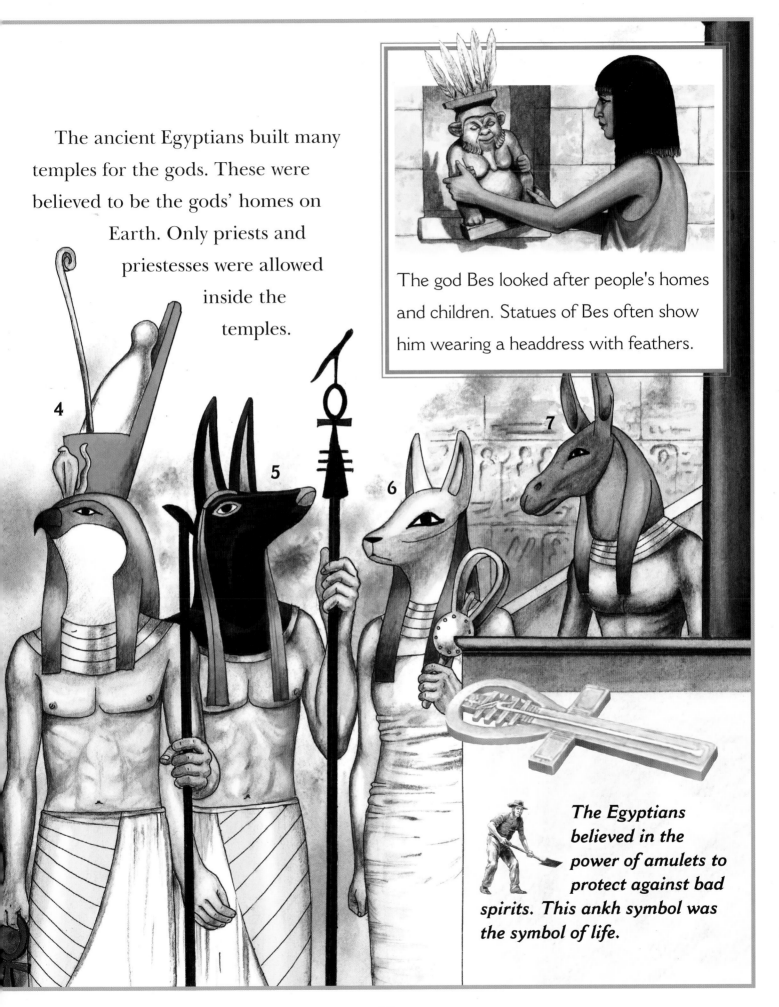

The god Bes looked after people's homes and children. Statues of Bes often show him wearing a headdress with feathers.

The Egyptians believed in the power of amulets to protect against bad spirits. This ankh symbol was the symbol of life.

The Story of Ra, the Sun God

One of the most important gods in ancient Egypt was Ra, the sun god. He was worshipped as the creator of everything, including all the gods and humans. He was also believed to be the father of all the pharaohs.

Ra is often shown with a hawk's head topped with a gold disk that looked like the sun, and with a cobra headdress.

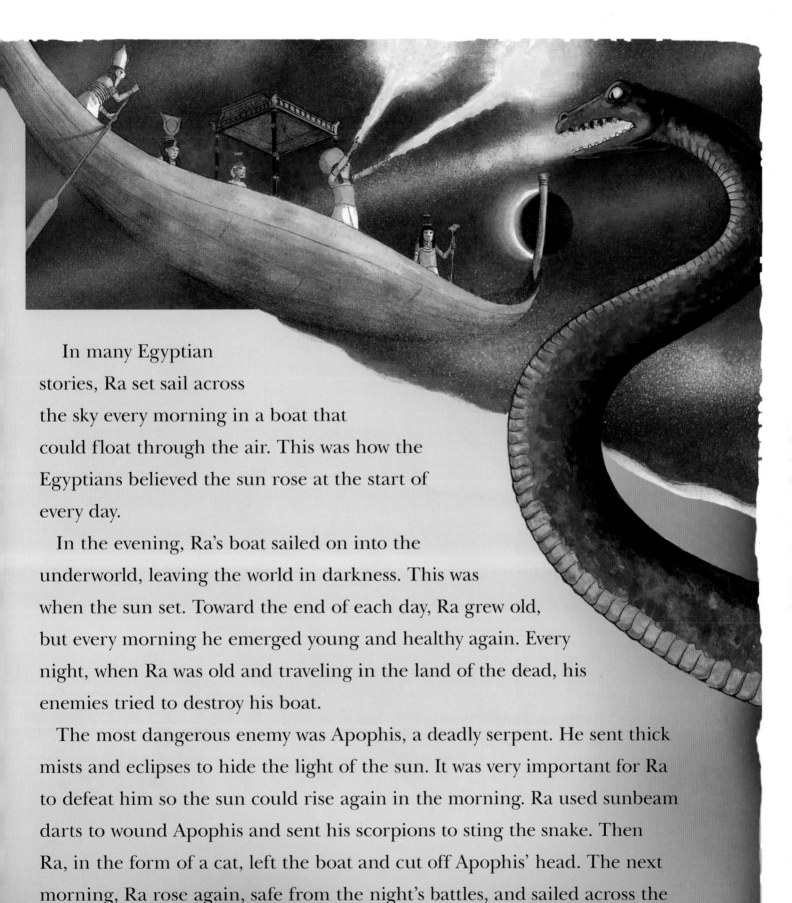

In many Egyptian
stories, Ra set sail across
the sky every morning in a boat that
could float through the air. This was how the
Egyptians believed the sun rose at the start of
every day.

In the evening, Ra's boat sailed on into the
underworld, leaving the world in darkness. This was
when the sun set. Toward the end of each day, Ra grew old,
but every morning he emerged young and healthy again. Every
night, when Ra was old and traveling in the land of the dead, his
enemies tried to destroy his boat.

The most dangerous enemy was Apophis, a deadly serpent. He sent thick
mists and eclipses to hide the light of the sun. It was very important for Ra
to defeat him so the sun could rise again in the morning. Ra used sunbeam
darts to wound Apophis and sent his scorpions to sting the snake. Then
Ra, in the form of a cat, left the boat and cut off Apophis' head. The next
morning, Ra rose again, safe from the night's battles, and sailed across the
sky on another of his daily voyages.

Amazing Mummies

The ancient Egyptians believed in life after death. For a dead person's soul to survive in the underworld, however, the person's body had to be preserved, or kept fresh. To stop bodies from rotting, the ancient Egyptians developed a process called mummification. The preserved dead bodies were called mummies.

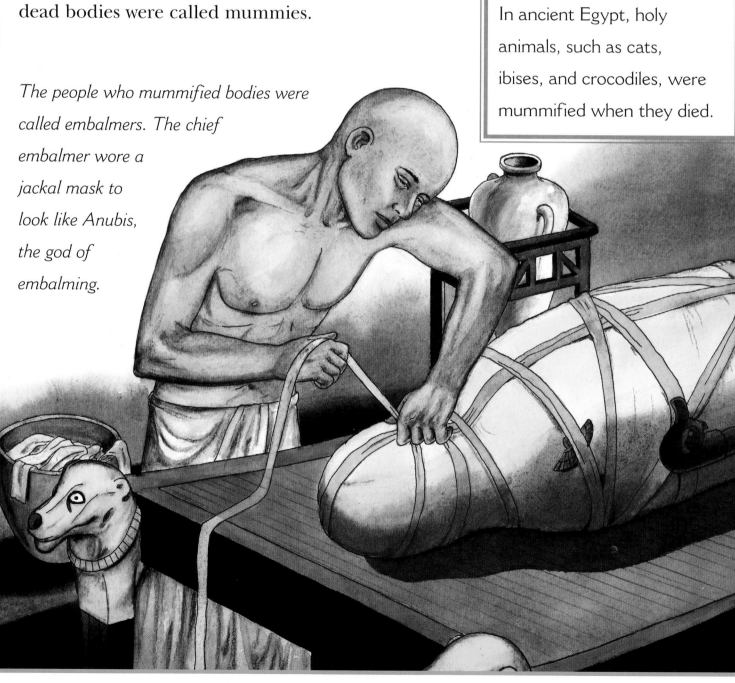

In ancient Egypt, holy animals, such as cats, ibises, and crocodiles, were mummified when they died.

The people who mummified bodies were called embalmers. The chief embalmer wore a jackal mask to look like Anubis, the god of embalming.

First, the body was washed, and the brain, liver, lungs, stomach, and intestines were removed. Next, the body was packed with salt to remove all the moisture. It was then stuffed with cloth or sawdust and sweet-smelling herbs, oiled, and wrapped in linen bandages, with amulets placed between the layers. Finally, it was placed inside a coffin.

Mummification was such a successful preservation method that many mummies are still intact today, thousands of years later.

Pyramids and Tombs

To shelter their bodies on their journey through the underworld, the Egyptian pharaohs had huge, pyramid-shaped tombs built for themselves. The slanting sides of the pyramid stood for the rays of the sun. The largest pyramid still standing is the Great Pyramid at Giza.

Millions of huge stone blocks were needed to build a pyramid. It took tens of thousands of builders to drag them into position using wooden sledges, rollers, and ramps.

The tombs of the pharaohs were filled with priceless treasures, including jewelry and furniture. This lured thieves, who looked for the tombs to steal what was in them.

Pharaohs who ruled later had their tombs dug deep into the cliff face in the Valley of the Kings. This was on the edge of the desert near the city of Thebes. A long tunnel led deep underground to the burial chamber. It was hoped that this would keep the tombs safe from thieves. Despite this, many tombs were robbed.

One of the most famous tombs ever found was that of the young king Tutankhamen. A beautiful golden death mask was placed over the mummy's face.

Arts and Crafts

Ancient Egyptian craft workers were highly skilled. They made beautiful pieces of pottery, jewelry, and furniture. They also made leather into sandals and soldiers' shields. Sons of craft workers usually followed their fathers into the family business. A skilled craft worker with his own workshop could make a good living.

Every city, town, and village had its own craft workers who made everyday items, like pots and baskets. Craft workers also worked in the temple workshops and made items for the pharaohs' palaces and tombs.

In ancient Egypt, mirrors were made from polished bronze or copper with metal or wooden handles. Some were placed in temples for use by the gods.

The wealthy wore necklaces, rings, and bracelets made from gold and colorful stones. Poorer people wore jewelry made of cheaper metals and stones.

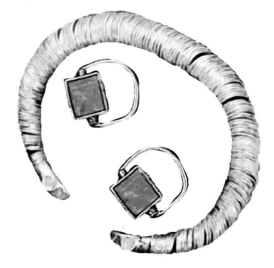

Many very fine pieces of gold jewelry have been found in the tombs of rich ancient Egyptians.

The Farming Year

Ancient Egypt's wealth was based on farming, and most Egyptians worked as farmers. They worked the fertile land left by the Nile's annual flood. Most people did not own any land themselves. They farmed large areas around the temples and land belonging to wealthy nobles. Part of their harvest was paid as tax to the pharaoh.

Farmers plowed their fields and sowed their seeds in November. The harvest began in March. From July to November, the fields were flooded, and all work stopped.

The most common crop grown in ancient Egypt was barley. Farmers also grew dates, grapes for making wine, and a wide range of fruits and vegetables.

A tool called a *shaduf* was used to move water from the river to the fields. It is still used in Egypt today.

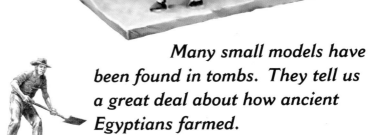

Many small models have been found in tombs. They tell us a great deal about how ancient Egyptians farmed.

Scribes and Schools

The ancient Egyptians used a kind of writing called hieroglyphs, in which each sign, or picture, stood for an object and a sound. Hieroglyphs were difficult to understand, and most people could not read or write. Professional writers, or scribes, were trained in special schools.

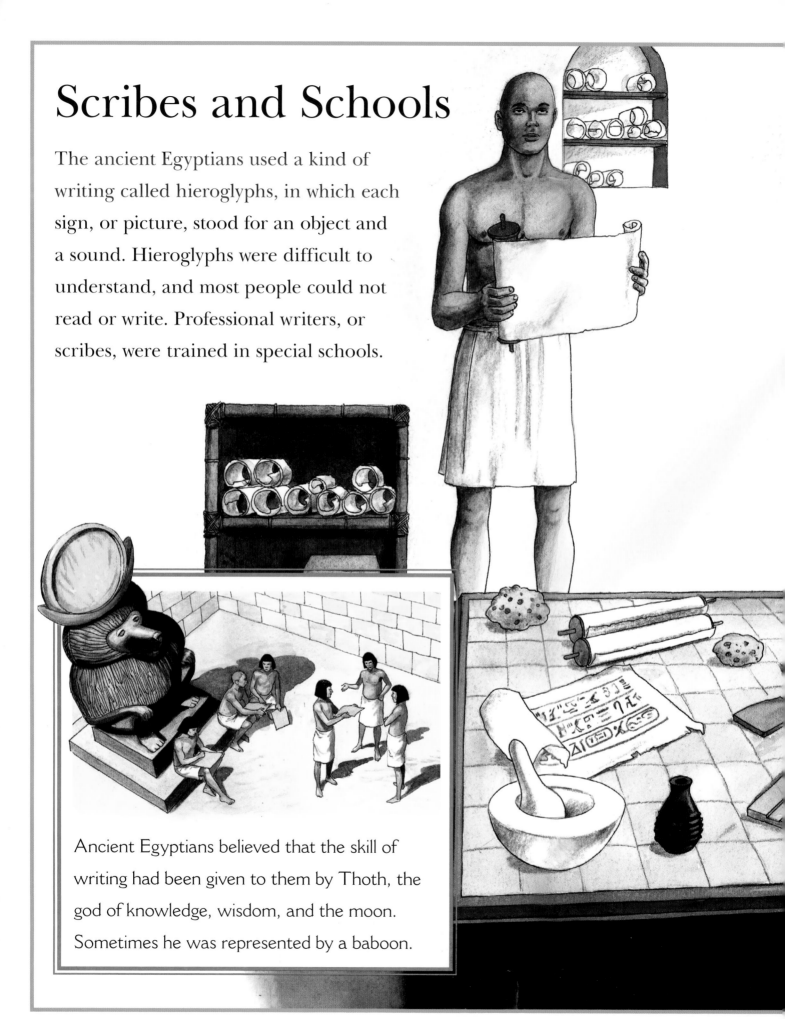

Ancient Egyptians believed that the skill of writing had been given to them by Thoth, the god of knowledge, wisdom, and the moon. Sometimes he was represented by a baboon.

Training began when a boy was about 9 years old, and it took up to 12 years to complete. Pupils had to work very hard, but it was well worth their effort. Good scribes were highly valued and were often rewarded with top jobs in the temples, army, law courts, or government.

The Rosetta Stone is covered with ancient writing. Its discovery allowed scholars to read Egyptian hieroglyphs.

Trainee scribes had to copy lines over and over. They practiced on broken pieces of pottery until they were good enough to be allowed to write on papyrus scrolls. Pens were made from reeds dipped in red or black ink.

Life at Home

Family life was important for ancient Egyptians. The father was head of the family, but women had many rights. How people lived depended on whether they were rich or poor. Wealthy Egyptians lived in large houses with lots of servants. Poor people worked long hours and enjoyed few luxuries.

The heads of ancient Egyptian boys were shaved except for long plaits called the locks of youth. At the age of 12, the boys' locks were cut off at a special ceremony to mark the start of their adult lives.

Beer was a very popular drink in ancient Egypt. It was made from bread mixed with water. It was strained to get rid of the lumps before serving.

Rich Egyptians liked to hold large banquets for their friends. They hired dancers and musicians to entertain their guests as they ate. Many types of food were served, including meat, fish, and a wide variety of fruits and vegetables.

In bed, the Egyptians used a cushion placed on a stand instead of a pillow. This allowed cool air to go around their heads as they slept.

Fun and Fashion

People worked hard in ancient Egypt, but they also found time to enjoy themselves. Hunting and wrestling were very popular sports. People also went to festivals for the gods that lasted several days, with singing, dancing, and street parades. Egyptian children liked to play with toys such as wooden dolls, animals on wheels, clay balls filled with seeds, and spinning tops.

A board for playing senet *was found in a tomb. Senet was a game played mostly by rich people, including the pharaohs.*

Ancient Egyptian nobles liked to go fishing and bird hunting in the marshes. They hurled sticks at the birds to stun them. Harpoons were used to catch fish. Noblemen hunted in the desert for antelope and hyenas.

Egyptian clothes were made from linen and were light and loose-fitting to keep people cool in the hot weather. Men wore loincloths or kilts. Women wore long dresses.

On special occasions, rich Egyptians liked to wear wigs of human hair or plant fiber.

What Happened to the Ancient Egyptians?

About 3,000 years ago, Egypt began to lose its power and was taken over by a series of foreign kings. Egyptian kings won back power several times, but always lost it again. Egypt was conquered by the Persians in the sixth century B.C. and again in the fourth century B.C.

With her Roman partner Mark Antony, Cleopatra
tried to keep Egypt independent. In 31 B.C., however, the
Romans defeated their soldiers at the Battle of Actium.

The Persians ruled until 2,300 years ago. Alexander the Great of Greece took Egypt from the Persians. After Alexander's death, his general, Ptolemy, took control and made himself king. He began a dynasty that ruled Egypt until 2,000 years ago, when it was taken over by the Romans.

Coins show the head of Queen Cleopatra VII, the last and most famous ruler of the Ptolemaic dynasty. She ruled from 51 to 30 B.C.

The sites of ancient Egypt attract many visitors. Statues guarding the temple of Abu Simbel were moved when the Aswan Dam was built on the Nile River.

Glossary

amulets—lucky charms worn to ward off bad luck and evil spirits

dynasty—a line of kings or queens from the same family

embalmers—people who prepared dead bodies for burial

fertile—land that is rich for growing crops

hieroglyphs—writing made up of pictures

ibises—a type of wading bird

linen—a type of cloth made from the fibers of the flax plant

loincloths—clothing worn by Egpyptian men, made from strips of cloth tied around their waists and passed between their legs

mummies—dead bodies that were prepared and wrapped in bandages, ready for burial

papyrus—a type of paper made out of reeds

pharaoh—the title given to the ruler of Egypt

pyramid—a tomb built for an ancient Egyptian ruler

scribes—highly trained, professional writers

scrolls—rolls of papyrus

Further Resources

AT THE LIBRARY

Fleming, Stuart. *The Egyptians.* New York: New Discovery Books, 1992.

Morley, Jacqueline. *How Would You Survive as an Ancient Egyptian?* New York: Franklin Watts, 1995.

Perl, Lila. *The Ancient Egyptians.* New York: Franklin Watts, 2004.

ON THE WEB

For more information on *Ancient Egyptians,* use FactHound to track down Web sites related to this book.

    1. Go to *www.facthound.com*

    2. Type in this book ID: 0756516455

    3. Click on the *Fetch It* button.

FactHound will find the best Web sites for you.

LOOK FOR MORE BOOKS IN THIS SERIES

ANCIENT CHINESE
ISBN 0-7565-1647-1

ANCIENT GREEKS
ISBN 0-7565-1646-3

ANCIENT MAYA
ISBN 0-7565-1677-3

ANCIENT ROMANS
ISBN 0-7565-1644-7

THE AZTECS
ISBN 0-7565-1950-0

THE INCAS
ISBN 0-7565-1951-9

THE VIKINGS
ISBN 0-7565-1678-1

Index